Please Don't Promise Me Forever

Please Don't Promise Me Forever

Photographs by
Rick Lyons

HALLMARK EDITIONS

Please don't promise me forever.

I want us to love each other

one day at a time...

...and string all those days together
like the precious things they are...

...instead of trying too hard
and promising too much.

Please don't expect me
to always be good and kind and loving.
There are times when I will be cold
and thoughtless
and hard to understand.

But it will only be because of the weather

or the flu

or one of my moods...

...not because I love you less.
Please remember that.

Please don't think about all the things
that could happen to us.
Don't think about other people
coming between us.
Don't think about outgrowing
each other or growing out of love.

Please *do* think about all the good things
that could happen to us.
Think of growing closer to each other,
finding new reasons for being together...

...and think of loving.

I will, too.

I am right now.

Please don't get mad at me
if I forget your birthday
or some special day we share...

...and please remember
that there is an "everydayness"
about what we have
that is beyond birthdays
and anniversaries.

That's why, sometimes,
I may not remember one special day...
because *all* our days are special
to me.

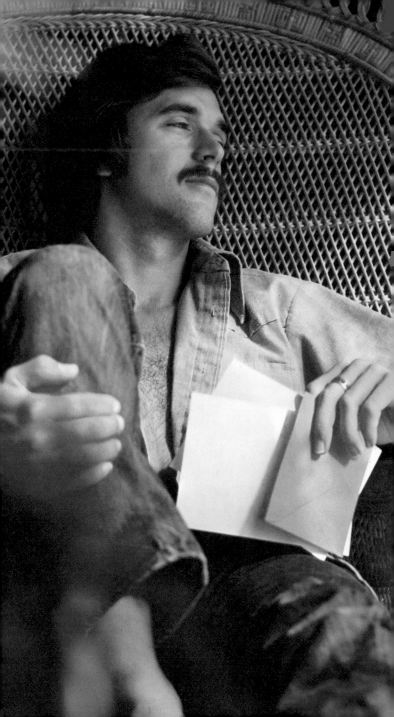

Please don't ever
sign a letter "as ever."

Please don't be too easy on me...
or expect me to be too easy on you.

Both of us have room to grow,
and both of us have to grow
if we want to hold each other's love.

Please don't ever give me
too much of yourself
or take too much of me.
In our togetherness
we still need our private places.

Please listen to me
when I'm talking to you...

...and please
don't ever think about someone else
when I kiss you.

Please don't start an argument
or make me look foolish
in front of other people...

...but when we're alone
don't feel like you're walking on eggs.
Go ahead and say what you think.
If I need telling off,
tell me off.

Then we can have our fight
and make up
and love again.
Just us.

Please remember
to call me sometimes
for no reason
except that you feel me thinking
about you,
needing your voice.

Please don't ever lose
that laugh of yours—
it's such a real laugh.

And never change the way
you brush my hair back from my eyes
and smile
when I'm trying to be very serious...
or the little odd ways you have
of saying things that make you "you,"
one of a kind,
the one I love.

Please
let's not use politeness
and busyness and silence
to avoid our problems
and the places where we hurt.
If something is wrong
let's go after it and make it right.

It's a good feeling
to think of growing older with you,
but, please,
let's not ever grow old.

I want us to always hang on
to the newness
that we have right now.
And let's never be ashamed
of our innocence,
of the child within us.
Let's never give up our dreams.

Please don't try to keep it from me
when you're feeling down.
I'll never be able to share your joy
if you try to protect me
from your sadness.

Please

don't ever say never...

...and please
don't promise me forever.
All I ask
is that you love me
now.

And please know
that I love you more
today
than I ever have before.
I can't promise you forever,
but I can promise you today
with the hope and belief
that there is a beautiful tomorrow
in store for us.

All my love

Karen

Set in Crown, designed exclusively
for Hallmark Editions by Hermann Zapf
and appearing for the first time in this book.
Printed on Hallmark Crown Royale paper.